Bill Gates

Bill Gates

Computer Programmer and Entrepreneur

LUCIA RAATMA

Ferguson
An imprint of Facts On File

Ferguson Career Biographies: Bill Gates

Ferguson
An imprint of Facts On File, Inc.
132 West 31st Street
New York NY 10001

Library of Congress Cataloging-in-Publication Data

Raatma, Lucia.
  Bill Gates : computer programmer and entrepreneur / by Lucia Raatma.
    p. cm. — (Ferguson's career biographies)
  Includes bibliographical references and index.
  Summary: A biography of the software developer and computer entrepreneur who founded Microsoft and helped make personal computers a reality.
  ISBN 0-89434-335-1
    1. Gates, Bill, 1955—Juvenile literature. 2. Businessmen—United States—Biography—Juvenile literature. 3. Computer software industry—United States—Juvenile literature. 4. Microsoft Corporation—History—Juvenile literature. [1. Gates, Bill, 1955–. 2. Businessmen. 3. Computer software industry. 4. Microsoft Corporation—History.] I. Series.

HD9696.63.U62 G375 2000
338.7'6100053'092—dc21
[B]   00-037592

An Editorial Directions Book.

Photographs ©: AP/Wideworld: Paul Sakuma 8; 22; Sal Veder 47; David A. Cantor 62; Greg Gibson 63; Lennox McLendon 65; Gary Stewart 71, 73; 89; John Todd 99; Archive: 10; Cobis: Lee Snider 26; 42, 46; Roger Ressmeyr 55, 67, 69; Anthony P. Bolante 93; W. Philpott 95; Liaison: 14; Diana Walker 39; Wolfgang Kaehler 50; Dirck Halstead 51, 52; Carol Halebian 59; Jeff Christensen 78, 81; Microsoft Archives: 15, 17, 23, 29, 33.

Printed in the United States of America

MP 10 9 8 7 6 4 5 3 2

This book is printed on acid-free paper.

CONTENTS

1 A COMPUTER IN EVERY HOME 9

2 A THING FOR COMPUTERS 13

3 THE CREATION OF MICROSOFT 25

4 MILLIONS AND BILLIONS 37

5 INFLUENCING THE WORLD 57

6 FATHERHOOD AND MORE 75

7 THE U.S. GOVERNMENT V. MICROSOFT 85

TIMELINE   101

HOW TO BECOME A
COMPUTER PROGRAMMER   103

TO LEARN MORE ABOUT
COMPUTER PROGRAMMERS   112

HOW TO BECOME AN
ENTREPRENEUR   114

TO LEARN MORE ABOUT
ENTREPRENEURS   121

TO LEARN MORE ABOUT
BILL GATES   123

INDEX   125

Bill Gates

Computers affect the lives of millions of people everyday, both at home and in the office.

A COMPUTER IN EVERY HOME

EVERY DAY, MILLIONS of people are affected by the work of Bill Gates. Each time a computer is turned on, each time a mouse is clicked, and each time the Internet is accessed, people are using the software that Gates helped develop.

Not long ago, computers were huge machines that took up entire rooms. Back in the 1960s and early 1970s, no one expected that anyone would want to use a computer at home. Only colleges, hospitals, government offices, and other large organizations used these complicated machines.

In the early days of computers, the machines were very large and could take up whole rooms.

But Bill Gates saw something else. He envisioned people using computers for everyday tasks. And he envisioned a computer in every home. As the years have passed, Gates's vision has become a reality.

Today, millions of people use personal computers, and millions more use computers in schools and offices.

Gates's work has made him famous, not to mention very wealthy. Some see him as a talented businessman. Others see him as greedy and aggressive. No matter how he is perceived, Bill Gates has changed the world we live in.

A THING FOR COMPUTERS

BILL GATES WAS A skinny and shy young man who was often uncomfortable around people. He preferred to read the encyclopedia or play card games for hours with his family. Later on, he would prefer the company of the computers he liked to build.

Beginnings

William H. Gates III was born on October 28, 1955, in Seattle, Washington, into a respected family. His father, William Gates Jr., was a well-known attorney in the com-

Bill Gates's father, William Gates Jr., didn't always understand his son's ambitions, but he always supported them.

munity. His mother, Mary, a schoolteacher, worked on numerous charitable committees and served as chairperson of the United Way.

As a boy, Bill was often called Trey, a common nickname for boys who had "III" as part of their name. A middle child, Bill had two sisters. Kristi was a year older, and Libby was nine years younger. In school, he did well in math and other courses requiring logic and analysis. But as a young boy, he never showed the leadership skills the world would later come to see.

Bill Gates and his sister, Libby

Always Thinking

When Bill was in the sixth grade, he and his mother were often at odds. She felt he should listen to her and do as he was told. But Bill had other ideas. One evening, after being called to dinner many times, Bill remained in his room. Finally, his mother asked over the intercom, "What are you doing?" He shouted back, "I'm thinking." "You're thinking?" she replied. "Yes, Mom, I'm thinking," he answered angrily. "Have you ever tried thinking?"

Conversations like this one eventually landed Bill in a counselor's office. His parents worried that they did not understand Bill and thought he needed someone else to talk to. In fact, Bill liked the psychologist they sent him to, and for a year he learned about psychology and various theories. However, at the end of that year, Mary Gates got this advice from the counselor: "You're going to lose. You had better adjust because there's no use trying to beat him." She began to accept that she had a strong-willed son.

A Young Programmer

Bill's education began in a public elementary school. Later he was enrolled in a private school called Lakeside. His best friend there was Kent Evans, a

Paul Allen (left) and Bill Gates at Lakeside in 1973

young man as intrigued by computers as Bill was. At one point, Bill remembered, "We read *Fortune* together; we were going to conquer the world."

Bill and Kent, along with their fellow schoolmate Paul Allen, formed a group called the Lakeside Programmers Group. Though they were very young, businessmen came to them with work. For example, one job required them to write a payroll system for a local company. Sometimes these friends would argue over their work. Bill always insisted on being the one in charge.

Today, parents and teachers alike would almost certainly praise Bill's interest in computers. At that time, however, computers did not play such a great part in people's lives because their uses were limited. The computer language of that day was called BASIC. Bill found one particularly mischievous use for his computer skills. He spent hours analyzing lines of code—program instructions—not only learning how a program worked, but also looking for its weaknesses. When he found a vulnerable spot in the computer code, he would alter it and disrupt the computer. To Gates, it was a kind of game. Gates found that he could also bypass security systems and thus get access to information that he wasn't supposed to have. This is called "hacking." Back then, there were no laws against hacking. Today, it is a serious crime.

Gates's high-school teachers did not find the young hacker's activities as amusing as Gates did, and he got into trouble at school. For some reason, though, the computer company that owned the systems he had hacked into from the school computers was not nearly as upset as his teachers. The company just wanted to know how Gates had broken into their system. How did a high-school kid manage to break into a system designed to keep out sophisticated adult hackers? The truth was that Gates had already mastered BASIC, and through his hacking, he had discovered a way to make mischief. Many hackers, like Bill, would later put their skills to good use writing computer programs. Hacking, though irritating to those whose computers were attacked, proved good training for a computer programmer.

In addition to programming, Bill's friend Kent enjoyed mountain climbing. But he had a tragic accident. One day he fell and was killed. Bill was devastated by Kent's death. As the weeks went by, Bill became closer to Paul. They spent a lot of time together and discussed all kinds of ideas. Their friendship, and their partnership, would last for years to come.

Gaining Independence

During his high-school years, Bill was struggling to figure out who he was. No doubt he felt out of place in his family at times. He also felt uncomfortable with other kids. His father recalled, "Trey didn't have a lot of confidence in social settings. I remember him fretting for two weeks before asking a girl to the prom, then getting turned down."

But Bill was always certain of his intelligence. He knew he was smart and felt he could do whatever he set his mind to. He remembers:

In ninth grade, I came up with a new form of rebellion. I hadn't been getting good grades, but I decided to get all A's without taking a book home. I didn't go to math class, because I knew enough and had read ahead, and I placed within the top ten people in the nation on an aptitude test. That established my independence and taught me I didn't need to rebel anymore.

While still in high school, Bill and Paul formed a company called Traf-O-Data, which analyzed city traffic patterns. They also wrote many computer programs, including one that handled class scheduling. During his senior year, Bill took some time off school and worked for a company called TRW. This government defense contractor needed computer programmers for some important projects, so they hired Bill and Paul. Bill enjoyed the job because he was able to work on his programming skills. Even as a teenager, Bill had a passion for programming and business.

In Washington, D.C.

In the summer of 1972, Bill was chosen to serve as a page in the U.S. Congress. He spent the summer running errands and doing office work for elected officials. But even with such minor responsibilities, Bill found a business opportunity.

Senator George McGovern was running for president at that time, and his choice for vice president was Senator Thomas Eagleton. But when details about Eagleton's mental health history became known, he resigned his candidacy. Obviously, the McGovern/Eagleton campaign buttons that had been produced were now worthless. But not to Bill. He bought up the old buttons and made a nice profit by selling them as collectors' items.

Senator Thomas P. Eagleton (left) and Senator George McGovern. Gates made money from the candidates' seemingly worthless campaign buttons.

Off to College

After graduating from Lakeside in 1973, Bill went to Harvard University. He intended to study law at Harvard in Cambridge, Massachusetts, and become an attorney like his father. But sometimes plans don't work out as expected. For Bill Gates, the future would be full of surprises.

Bill Gates graduating from Lakeside.

THE CREATION OF MICROSOFT

L IFE AT HARVARD was different for Gates. At Lakeside, he had really stood out as the brightest student. At Harvard, however, he was simply another smart person. Even though he earned a perfect score on the math section of the SAT, Gates found that some students at Harvard knew more about math than he did.

A Computer Career

Gates spent most of his time at Harvard playing card and arcade games and continuing his computer programming. His grades

On the Harvard campus. When Gates went to college, he discovered that he was "just another smart guy."

were fine, but he never studied. He was attracted to applied mathematics because it offered a way to use math for practical purposes, such as computers. He spent hours and hours at the computer center on campus, and he tried to think of a way to make a career for himself out of working with computers. But he didn't have much of a social life. He would only attend parties when his friend Steve Ballmer dragged him to them.

Gates could often be found in the Harvard University computer labs, where he was remembered as not such a nice guy. His belief that he was smarter than other people often led him to criticize other students sharply. And this was not his only problem adjusting to life on campus. His grades suffered because his attention to games left little time for academic pursuits. The card playing gave Gates an escape from the pressures of his freshman year, and the video games helped to spark his imagination.

At the end of his freshman year, he withdrew from school because of illness. After he recovered, he returned to school—and then dropped out a few more times. The great institution of learning proved not to be the place where Gates would express his particular genius. Finally, he dropped out of school altogether before graduation.

During his second year at Harvard, Gates began to get clearer ideas about his future. One day, Paul Allen, who was working for Honeywell outside Boston, showed him a magazine cover that changed everything. The magazine was *Popular Electronics,* and it featured a computer called Altair 8800. This computer was made by MITS (Micro Instrumentation and Telemetry Systems), a company based in Albuquerque, New Mexico. The Altair was the first device to be called a personal computer—a familiar term today—and it was sold at an affordable price.

"Look," Allen said as he showed Gates the article. "It's going to happen! . . . And we are going to miss it." Gates sat down and read about this new piece of hardware. And he thought about his friend's words. This was a chance he was not going to miss.

Working with the Altair

Computer enthusiasts across the United States were excited about the arrival of the Altair. However, the machine was really just a box with lights and toggle switches. It was nothing like the computers used

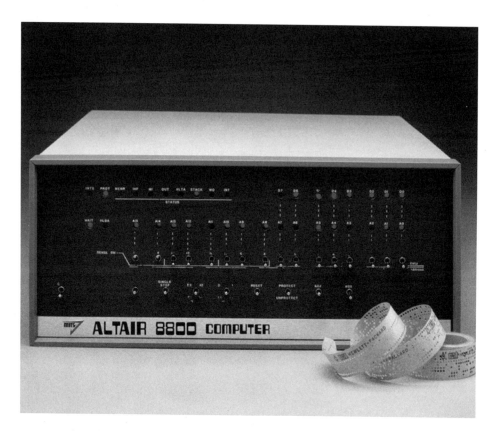

The Altair 8800 computer

today. It had neither a keyboard nor a display screen, so there was little it could do. Allen and Gates decided to change that.

The two young men called Ed Roberts, the owner of MITS, and told him that they wanted to create a program—a language for the Altair. They implied that they had already written a version of BASIC to run his computer, but actually they had just begun to think about it.

When Roberts expressed interest, they were ecstatic. For eight weeks, Gates and Allen spent nearly every waking moment working on the software. They fell asleep writing code and started writing code again as soon as they woke up. Gates skipped many classes to meet the deadline that had been set. Gates has said, "I have a soft spot in my heart for BASIC. It was Microsoft's first product, written in my college dorm room."

Finally, Gates and Allen arranged to bring the new program to Roberts. Because money was tight, only one of them could fly to Albuquerque for the meeting. Allen was given this honor because he looked older than Gates did.

When he arrived at the MITS office, Allen worried about how the software would perform. Back at Harvard, Gates was worried too. Since they had written the program without having an actual Altair computer to use, they were afraid that the software might not work. But they had improvised well. As Gates later remembered, "One little mistake would have meant the program wouldn't have run. The first time we tried it was at MITS, and it came home without a glitch."

The Altair was now a usable machine—and the future of the computer industry had been forever changed. Gates and Allen had started something big.

The Next Step

After that success, Allen was offered a job at MITS. So in March 1975, he moved to Albuquerque. Gates stayed on at Harvard, but his life was not the same. He and Allen knew they had much to offer to this growing industry.

After Gates finished his second year of college, he went to Albuquerque for the summer. He and Allen had decided to start their own company. In those summer months, Microsoft was born, though that name was not decided upon until November of that year.

The company name was a combination of the words "microcomputer" and "software." At first, it was spelled Micro-soft, but later the hyphen was dropped. Little did the two entrepreneurs know that Microsoft would grow into one of the world's most recognized trademarks.

Software Licensing

When Allen and Gates sold their version of BASIC for the Altair, they had signed a licensing agreement with MITS. Under this agreement, they would make money from the sale of their software whether it was sold as part of the Altair or sold separately. This agreement was the beginning of Gates's concern over software theft. Computer hobbyists often copied the software they used and gave it to their friends for free. However, Gates believed that all users should pay for the software they used.

Keynote Speaker

In March 1976, MITS sponsored the World Altair Computer Convention in Albuquerque. Altair owners, dealers, and programmers—virtually everyone interested in the new technology was at the convention. And serving as keynote speaker to the group was twenty-year-old Bill Gates.

Moving Ahead

In late 1976, Paul Allen quit his job with MITS to work full-time for Microsoft. Meanwhile, Gates had been trying to license their version of BASIC with General Electric, NCR, Citibank, and many other corporations. By the beginning of 1977, he knew what his life's work would be. He dropped out of Harvard and moved to New Mexico to join Paul.

Gates remembers his parents' reaction: "My parents weren't all that excited about their son announcing he was dropping out of a fine university

The Albuquerque group in 1978

to start a business in something almost nobody had ever heard of called 'microcomputers.' But they were always very supportive."

Microsoft's first office was located at Two Park Central Tower in Albuquerque. While there, the company continued a battle that had begun with MITS. Gates and Allen felt they should have the right to sell their software to anyone who wanted it, while MITS wanted the exclusive rights. A court ruled in Microsoft's favor. Shortly thereafter, MITS had financial problems and closed down.

In the meantime, Microsoft was developing a second computer language. An IBM team developed FORTRAN in 1956. Microsoft adapted the language for a new computer chip, called the 8080, which it shipped in July 1977. Again Microsoft had taken someone else's invention and made it more usable. This practice would occur often in the years to come. Allen spent most of his time developing the software, while Gates negotiated deals with other companies.

Gates and Allen had changed the way in which the Altair could be used. Gates was eager to share his vision of personal computing with the public.

Taking Risks

As a young man, Gates enjoyed downhill skiing, and he took the slopes with great speed. Over the years, Gates has become known for his fast and reckless driving. Often not wearing a seatbelt, he zooms along roads and through streets. This daredevil manner is dangerous, but it is definitely part of his personality. He is not afraid to try anything, no matter how risky.

Heading Home

By 1978, Gates and Allen decided to move the Microsoft office. They felt that Albuquerque was too isolated, and they wanted to return to the Northwest. In early 1979, new offices were set up in Bellevue, Washington. Microsoft had a new home.

MILLIONS AND BILLIONS

4

ICROSOFT GREW RAPIDLY after moving to Bellevue. The company hired more employees, and sales of its software mushroomed. For all its success, however, everything at Microsoft was not perfect. Important deadlines were missed and sometimes products were not as well designed as they might have been. But Bill Gates was still driven to be the first on the market. He wanted the software to be shipped quickly, saying that it could be fine-tuned by programmers later.

In spite of its imperfections, however,

Microsoft was having a real impact on the computer-conscious public. Its version of BASIC was available on nearly every personal computer made.

Taking on the World

Microsoft entered the Japanese market in 1978. In 1979, they expanded their international sales by entering the European market. The company began working with computer manufacturers to build their hardware. The Microsoft name was quickly becoming known throughout the world.

Keeping Up

In 1979, Intel introduced the 8086 chip. It was a new microprocessor that worked twice as fast as the old ones. Gates and Allen, knowing that they had to keep up with this technology, decided to create a new version of BASIC that would run with the 8086 chip. Their new software was introduced at the National Computer Conference in New York City in June 1979.

The Competition

Many other companies were trying to make progress in this new computer industry. Apple Com-

Steve Jobs in 1982. He was the head of Apple Computer, which was Microsoft's main competitor.

puter, a company run by Steve Jobs and Steve Wozniak, was Microsoft's main competitor. Jobs was a true visionary, and he had many unique ideas about how computers could influence the world. Jobs was and continues to be a very creative man. In fact, there have been times when Gates has no doubt been envious of Jobs's inventiveness. But at other times, Jobs's good ideas have led to even better ideas from Gates.

Gates offered to sell BASIC to Apple at one point, but Apple turned the offer down. Jobs and Wozniak felt they could write their own software, and they were sure it would be easier to use than BASIC.

Gates and Allen got a look at the projects Apple was working on, and this led to another Microsoft product—the SoftCard. At first, Apple computers could use only Apple software. But the SoftCard allowed Apple computers to run other programs. This 1980 invention proved quite profitable for Microsoft.

Working with an Old Friend

In June 1980, Steve Ballmer left his job with Proctor & Gamble and went to work at Microsoft. Ballmer, Gates's friend from Harvard, signed on as first assistant to the president. He took on many of the administrative tasks that Gates had been trying to handle. Ballmer also hired some very good people for the company.

Gates was delighted that Ballmer had joined his organization. As he explained later, "I always knew I would have close business associates like Ballmer and several of the other top people at Microsoft, and that we would stick together and grow together no matter what happened. I didn't know that because of some analysis. I just decided early on [it] was part of who I was."

A New Idea

At this point technology was changing rapidly in the computer industry. Computer users had many new tasks for the computers, and new programs for accounting and word processing needed to be written. With this in mind, Microsoft began to create software that anyone could buy right off a computer store shelf.

A Deal with IBM

International Business Machines (IBM) approached Microsoft for a big project in July 1980. IBM had

Inspecting typewriters at the IBM plant. IBM had long been known for producing typewriters and other office machines.

long been a leader in technology. They manufactured typewriters and a wide variety of other office machines. They asked Microsoft to write an operating system for a computer they were working on. IBM had begun to realize that there was a big future in personal computers, and they wanted to enter that market.

The fact that IBM came to Bill Gates was somewhat ironic. Sometimes Gates had seen the corporate giant as the enemy, and his personal style was quite unlike that of an IBM executive. Gates was known for dressing casually, if not sloppily, and for leaving his hair uncombed. Meeting with IBM could be intimidating, but Gates was up to the challenge.

The computer IBM was developing was top secret, and they asked Microsoft not to discuss the project with anyone else. Creating an operating system for IBM was a big job, and Gates was a little worried about the task. Though the partnership would bring success to Microsoft, the deadline for IBM was only one year away. Gates knew that the project would be a lot of work for his people.

With this in mind, Bill Gates did something very smart—or some would say very sneaky. He knew that a software program they could use might already exist. He spoke to Seattle Computer Products about their 86-QDOS program, explaining that he had a potential client for it. Gates never said the client was IBM, because he was afraid that Seattle Computer would go directly to IBM, and Microsoft would be out of the picture.

Seattle Computer Products agreed to sign a contract with Microsoft. The agreement gave Microsoft nonexclusive rights to their operating system. Bill Gates had found a way to provide for IBM's needs while saving a critical amount of time.

Closing the Deal

When Gates and his team met with the IBM executives to finalize the details of the deal, there was much to discuss. One issue Gates felt strongly about was retaining rights to the operating system they were providing. IBM had not considered how much money can be made from software sales, so they agreed to Gates's demands. Gates also insisted that Microsoft receive royalties, a monetary percentage, for each IBM computer sold with the Microsoft operating system. The twenty-four-year-old knew just what he wanted.

Developing MS-DOS

In the months that followed, IBM continued to work on their personal computer. And Microsoft worked on revising 86-QDOS for IBM's needs. The Microsoft staff worked many hours of overtime in order to complete the project, and everyone kept the secret they had been sworn to.

What Microsoft ultimately created was called MS-DOS. The term DOS stands for *disk operating system*. Not knowing what they had provided, Seattle Computer Products sold Microsoft exclusive rights to their system for a mere $50,000. Finally, in August 1981, IBM introduced its personal computer to the world. Loaded on each computer was MS-DOS from Microsoft.

International Success

The release of MS-DOS and the partnership with IBM catapulted Microsoft to the top of the computer software market. The sales of MS-DOS brought in up to $200 million a year for Microsoft. Additionally Microsoft made more money from each computer sold by IBM. The financial results were truly astounding.

One of IBM's first personal computers. This PC came loaded with software from Microsoft.

Continued Competition

Bill Gates could not help noticing that Steve Jobs and Apple Computer continued to make strides in computer technology. He was curious about their projects and eager to see their inventions at work.

Apple innovations. Steve Jobs (left), John Scully (center), and Steve Wozniak of Apple unveiled a new line of computers in 1984.

At one point, Gates and Jobs, along with some of their employees, met to share ideas. Gates learned much about Jobs's ideas and offered to produce software for them to use. Some say the products that Microsoft subsequently created were the results of competitive collaboration. Others accused Gates of stealing ideas from Apple. In any case, Microsoft's software continued to improve.

Word, Windows, and the Mouse

In the next few years, Microsoft created products that changed the way computers worked. In 1983, the company introduced Microsoft Word, an advanced word-processing program. That same year, it introduced Windows, a new program that allowed users to work on more than one document or program at once. This was quite an innovation. And the mouse, the handheld device so common today, allowed users to point at and click on the information they needed. The lines and lines of commands that had to be typed on a computer screen were long gone.

Losing a Friend

But along with all the success for Bill Gates came bad news. His close friend and confidante, Paul

Allen, was diagnosed with Hodgkin's disease, a type of cancer. Allen had been a very important part of the birth of Microsoft and had supported Gates in many projects over the years.

When he learned of his illness, Allen knew he had to change his life. He decided it was time to reevaluate his priorities, to step back and take a look at himself. In February 1983, Allen, who was then executive vice president, resigned from Microsoft. Some say he left on bad terms and that he and Gates did not speak for years. But no matter what the circumstances of his resignation, Allen returned several years later to serve on the board of directors.

An Anniversary

Microsoft celebrated its ten years of business in 1985. Over that time, it had grown rapidly. What had started as an idea thought up by two young men had become a leading business that employed 900 people. Its annual sales had reached $140 million, and the future appeared to be full of possibility.

Moving to the Campus

The success of Microsoft meant the company needed more employees and more space. So in

Miscrosoft campus. The company moved to this Redmond, Washington, location in 1986.

1986, it moved to Redmond, Washington, to a place called Corporate Campus. The site consists of forty-one buildings and covers 270 acres (109 hectares). The complex has a pond in the center, walking paths, and a softball field.

Microsoft's employees are mostly young people and they dress casually. But their approach to their

Gates and some of his employees. Casual dress is an accepted part of the Microsoft lifestyle.

jobs is anything but casual. They work long hours and their loyalty to Bill Gates drives their dedication. As their leader, Gates pushes his employees. He seems to want the best products and to be the first one to have them to sell. No matter what, he wants Microsoft to be on top. He hates to lose.

Gates once explained about his employees and his company, "If we weren't still hiring great people and pushing ahead, it would be easy to fall behind and become a mediocre company. Fear should guide you, but it should be latent. I consider failure on a regular basis."

Microsoft employees are well rewarded for working so hard. Company picnics and lavish holiday parties are held every year.

As a Leader

Bill Gates is a ferocious leader, but his approach to business situations is unique. His meetings are really discussions, and he listens to the ideas of the people who work for him. However, he is quick to judge those who aren't up to his standards: "That's the stupidest thing I've ever heard of," he's been known to say. A former staff member once said, "You'd hate him some days and love him some days,

The people at Microsoft work hard, but they know how to play hard too.

but he'd always push you to be better than you were the day before."

Before giving up his role as chief executive officer of Microsoft, Gates's style was to keep in touch with the people who work for him. He wrote hundreds of e-mail messages every day, responding directly to ideas and questions. He held monthly meetings with top management. And he spent most of his time running small review sessions, in which he met with teams of people from various divisions of the company who were working on various projects.

One quirk Gates is known for is rocking back and forth. This habit began when he was a young boy and he was given a rocking horse. He would rock on the horse for hours. Now, when he is thinking or concentrating, he rocks back and forth in his chair. People at Microsoft became quite used to seeing their leader thinking, listening, and rocking as he sat in at meetings.

Going Public

Up until 1986, Microsoft was a privately held company. But that year, Gates decided to go public. This means that he was willing to sell shares in Microsoft to people outside the company. The first day Microsoft shares were available on Wall Street, the company earned $61 million. And thirty-one-year-old Bill Gates became a multimillionaire. Within one year, he would become a billionaire.

In 1986, Bill Gates was recognized by PC Magazine *as the person having the greatest impact on the computer industry that year.*

INFLUENCING
THE WORLD

N THE YEARS that followed, Bill Gates found himself at odds with IBM executives. IBM was working hard on a new computer system, called the PC/AT. Again, IBM wanted Microsoft to design its software. However, Gates was not sure if IBM's new hardware would be a success.

Windows 2.0

Microsoft agreed to design a software package called OS/2 for IBM. However, at the same time, Microsoft programmers were working on Windows 2.0, a revised version of the original Windows. This new version would work with a faster microchip that Intel built.

IBM felt that Windows 2.0 would be in direct competition with OS/2. The company was angry that Microsoft felt no loyalty to them. In the end, IBM's new system was not very successful, and it was also very expensive. When Windows 2.0 was introduced in 1988, it was a huge hit. And Gates immediately set his people to work on an even better version.

Windows 3.0

In 1990, Windows 3.0 was introduced. This software was not compatible with IBM's OS/2, which again made IBM angry. This newest version was even easier to use than the previous releases, so for the first time it proved to be serious competition for the Macintosh computers built by Apple. At the time, Apple had a reputation for creating systems that were easy for even beginners to learn. But now, Windows was just as easy to use.

In 1990, Microsoft celebrated its fifteenth anniversary as a company. That year, its sales reached $1-billion.

As Windows was updated over the years, it became more user friendly and efficient.

Facing Lawsuits

As Bill Gates's success grew, his competition found much to complain about. In 1988, Apple Computer, which claimed that the idea for Windows was stolen from their designs, sued Microsoft. Gates agreed that there were similarities between the two systems, but he argued that there were also differences. After five years and much debate, Apple lost the lawsuit. But along the way, Bill Gates and Microsoft made some enemies.

Gates is often defensive about the charges that have been made against him. He once argued, "Those are clear lies. Who grew this market? We did. Who survived companies like IBM, ten times our size, taking us on?" Gates seems to feel that leaders at other companies are as competitive as he is, just not as successful.

Over the years, Microsoft has faced other legal issues. Many people feel that Gates and Microsoft have created a monopoly in the market. The Federal Trade Commission has investigated the situation and more action may be taken. A judge ruled that Microsoft must be divided into smaller companies. But for now, Microsoft remains one of the most powerful corporations in the world.

More Innovations

Under Gates's leadership, Microsoft made some amazing inventions in the early 1990s. One was the Microsoft BallPoint Mouse, introduced in 1991 to work with laptop computers. This allowed people who used laptops the same freedom that desktop computer users had. They were finally able to move across a computer screen in an easier way.

Progress was also made in multimedia. In 1993, Microsoft Encarta was made available. This multimedia encyclopedia contained a huge collection of articles—complete with illustrations, photos, movies, maps, animations, and sounds—and is all on one CD-ROM. No longer did an encyclopedia have to be a collection of expensive and cumbersome books. The same information found in forty-volume encyclopedias was now available on a single CD-ROM. This format was much easier to update and cost a lot less.

Also in 1993, Microsoft developed Mouse 2.0. This new version of the Mouse had several new features and was designed to work well for both left-handed and right-handed users. And in late 1993, Microsoft was named by *Fortune* magazine as the "Most Innovative Company Working in the United States."

Microsoft created many different kinds of software, including programs that could write checks and keep track of other financial matters.

National Medal of Technology

In 1992, Bill Gates received an honor from President George H.W. Bush. At a ceremony in the White House Rose Garden, Gates was awarded the National Medal of Technology for Technological

In 1992, President Bush awarded Gates with the National Medal of Technology for Technological Achievement.

Achievement. President Bush praised Gates and explained that the recognition was "for his early vision of universal computing at home and in the office, for his technical and business management skills in creating a worldwide technology company, and for his contribution to the development of the personal computing industry."

Time Out for a Personal Life

In 1987, Bill Gates met Melinda French at a Microsoft company picnic. She worked in his marketing department and later became an executive. They dated for the next several years. On New Year's Day 1994, Gates and French were married.

Their wedding, which took place in Hawaii, was a private affair. The celebration cost more than $1 million. Among those in attendance were four billionaires: Gates himself, Microsoft cofounder Paul Allen, Microsoft vice president Steve Ballmer, and Gates's friend Warren Buffet, chairman of a huge clothing and investment company.

As odd as it may sound, Gates used his money in hopes of making his wedding more "normal." It is said that he booked all the hotel rooms on the Hawaiian island and hired all the helicopters—just

Melinda French was an employee at Microsoft before she married its famous founder.

so the photographers would have to stay away. Katherine Graham, a guest at the wedding and publisher of the *Washington Post*, remarked, "They really wanted a private, human wedding and they didn't want publicity. They didn't want people with cameras and notebooks. I respected their wishes."

Since their marriage, Melinda Gates has left Microsoft. Now she concentrates on charity work and serves on the board of directors of Duke University. She is smart and independent, but also friendly and outgoing.

A Palace Fit for a King

In the mid 1990s, Bill Gates also focused some of his efforts on building a new home. Not just any new house would do. The house was built on Lake Washington in Medina, Washington, not far from the Microsoft headquarters.

The 40,000-square-foot (103,600-square-meter) home includes a thirty-car garage, a swimming pool complete with an underwater stereo system, a large library, a movie theater, and a dining room that seats 150. It has huge vaulted ceilings and unique collections of artwork. One room has a trampoline, because Gates enjoys jumping as much as rocking.

The Gates home on Lake Washington in Medina. It features a 30 car garage, a swimming pool, a movie theater, and 150-seat dining room.

Unique Friendships

It might seem odd that Bill Gates is friendly with Warren Buffet, a man who is about twenty years older than Gates. Buffet used to be the richest man in the United States, before Gates passed him up. Yet their friendship really has nothing to do with money. The two share common interests and enjoy spending time with each other. They often vacation together and they both like card games. As businessmen, Buffet and Gates may have a friendly rivalry. But mostly they respect one another and have learned much from each other. Gates has commented, "I think Warren has had more effect on the way I think about my business and the way I think about running it than any other business leader."

Another special friend for Gates is Ann Winblad, a software entrepreneur Gates dated in the 1980s. Because they were both very busy during that time, they were often in different cities. So sometimes they would have "virtual dates." They would go to the same movie on the same night, but in different places, and discuss it by phone later.

Winblad and Gates broke up in 1987. She was eager for marriage, and he was not yet ready. But when he decided to marry Melinda French, Gates spoke to Winblad about it and got her blessing. Today, Winblad and Gates remain good friends and often vacation together.

As Winblad explained, "We share our thoughts about the world and ourselves. And we marvel about how, as two young overachievers, we began a great adventure on the fringes of a little-known industry and it landed us at the center of an amazing universe."

Ann Winblad, a software entrepreneur, once dated Gates and is now considered a close friend.

A Very Big Year

In 1995, Microsoft celebrated its twentieth anniversary. At that point, the company employed more than 16,350 people. And nothing appeared to be slowing down.

In March, the company announced a partnership with the new movie studio DreamWorks SKG. Their agreement was to design interactive and multimedia entertainment products.

This agreement with such a large entertainment company was a sign of the times. More and more large companies have been joining forces in the entertainment world. Publishing houses and movie studios, newspaper companies and television networks—so many are working together to provide unique entertainment products for the public.

Softimage, which is a smaller company within Microsoft, has worked with DreamWorks on a number of ideas over the years. Together they developed Directors' Chair, which is a real-time digital scene-editing tool. Softimage has also provided the technology for computer-generated animation that is used by DreamWorks.

In August, Microsoft introduced Windows 95, the

Bill Gates with filmmaker Steven Spielberg (right), cofounder of DreamWorks SKG

next version of Windows. The new product was celebrated with parties, TV commercials, and many media events. Within four days, more than 1 million copies of the software had been sold in North America. By October, more than 7 million copies had been sold worldwide.

Also in 1995, Microsoft launched the Microsoft Network, a full-service Internet-service provider. Within three months of the launch, more than 500,000 members enrolled.

In November of that year, Bill Gates published a book called *The Road Ahead*. The book outlined his views on technology and how new innovations would influence the way people work, play, and live. It held the number one spot on the *New York Times* best-seller list for seven weeks.

At year's end, Microsoft made more progress in the Internet and on television. The company introduced a new version of Microsoft Internet Explorer, an advanced Internet browser. Microsoft also joined forces with NBC and created two new businesses—a twenty-four-hour news channel called MSNBC and an interactive online news service. Microsoft appeared to influence every corner of the world.

At the launch of Windows 95. Within four days, more that 1 million copies of the software were sold in North America.

FATHERHOOD
AND MORE

I N 1996, BILL and Melinda Gates became the happy parents of a daughter, Jennifer Katherine. Three years later, they had a son, Rory John. In many ways, Gates's life continued as it had before their two children were born. In many other ways, it was never to be the same.

Since becoming a father, Gates has become more introspective about his and Microsoft's many contributions to the world of computing. Bill Gates continues to consider what the future may hold for the next generation:

Everyone starts out really capable. But as you grow and turn curious, either you get positive feedback by finding answers or you don't, and then this incredible potential you have is discouraged. I was lucky. I always had a family and resources to get more and more answers. Digital tools will allow a lot more people to keep going to the next step rather than hitting a wall where people stop giving them information or tell them to stop asking questions.

At Microsoft

In the years following his marriage and the beginnings of fatherhood, Gates has continued to work hard in his leadership of Microsoft. New products have been introduced at a rapid pace—Windows 98, and new versions of Internet Explorer, as well as plans for Windows 2000—and Gates has remained at the top of the market and ahead of everyone else.

In 1997, the company even announced a collaboration with Apple. This partnership came as a surprise to many because of the ill will that had existed between Gates and Steve Jobs of Apple. However, the two companies agreed to work together on a number of projects.

No matter what their past history had been, Gates and Jobs realized that their products would be better if they worked together. Microsoft agreed to develop many of its tools for Mac users, while Apple agreed to make Microsoft's Internet Explorer the default browser for its new software.

Some accused Steve Jobs of "selling out" to the powerful Bill Gates, but others understood how practical the arrangement was. Jobs said of the partnership, "We are thrilled at the prospect of working more closely with Microsoft on applications and Internet software. We are confident that this is the beginning of a much closer relationship between the two companies, which will greatly benefit our common customers."

Giving Back

As his billions have grown, Bill Gates has become dedicated to using his money for good causes. Together with his wife, he founded the Bill and Melinda Gates Foundation, an organization that works to bring learning and health to all the people of the world. At present, the foundation has committed more than $300 million to global health; more than $300 million to education, bringing com-

Bill and Melinda Gates created a charitable organization that works to improve learning and health all over the world.

puters and Internet access to less prosperous people throughout the United States and Canada; more than $54 million to community projects in the Pacific Northwest; and more than $29 million to special projects and other charity campaigns.

Gates explained, "Giving is a complex thing. You have to find things you really believe in and that are fun to give to. I take philanthropy very seriously and I am learning about it." Bill and Melinda Gates hope the money they have earned through their work will help to improve the lives of others.

Educating "Generation I"

To Bill Gates, children born in the 1990s belong to "Generation I," the Internet generation. He feels that the Internet will affect their lives just as dramatically as the invention of television affected the lives of "Baby Boomers" (those born in the 1950s and early 1960s).

In October 1999, Gates addressed the New York Institute of Technology. During that speech, he urged teachers to keep up with the new technology so that they could better educate their students. "The Internet will change education as fundamentally as it changed with printed books," he said. "We have a responsibility to make sure every teacher is able to use this technology to help 'Generation I' learn."

After this speech, Gates was given the President's Medal Leadership Award from the New York Institute of Technology. This annual award is given to those who make outstanding contributions to the fields of technology and education.

Free Time

In recent years, Gates has tried to spend more time with his family enjoying simpler things. He likes reading and playing bridge, and he even took up golf. But as longtime friend and colleague Steve Ballmer said, "Bill got into golf in the same addictive way he gets into anything else. It gets his competitive juices flowing."

Author Again

In 1999, Bill Gates published another book, *Business @ the Speed of Thought*. This work explained how business problems can be solved by digital processes. Gates feels that in order for businesses to succeed in this fast-paced economy, they must enable the flow of digital information.

Business @ the Speed of Thought received a great

Signing copies of Business @ the Speed of Thought *for students in a London bookstore*

deal of attention and critical praise. It also earned spots on the best-seller lists of the *New York Times*, *USA Today*, the *Wall Street Journal*, and Amazon.com. Gates donated the proceeds from this book as well as those from *The Road Ahead* to nonprofit groups that work to bring technology to education.

Stepping Aside

In early 2000, Bill Gates did something that took many people by surprise. He announced that he was stepping down as chairman and chief operating officer of Microsoft. Steve Ballmer was named to replace him.

By making this move, Gates explained that he wished to spend more time in software development. "I am returning to what I love most—focusing on technologies for the future," he said. Gates remains prominent at Microsoft however, still serving as chairman of the board.

Looking Back and Looking Ahead

No doubt, Bill Gates has come a long way from the young man at Lakeside with a passion for computers. However, his image has changed over the years. At first, he appeared to be an eccentric, unkempt entrepreneur. Then he was seen as a software wizard, a leader in the new technology. And later he was perceived by his competitors to be ruthless and aggressive.

Today, the world's richest man still has big ideas for the future. He sees ways in which his wealth can help those around him and other people throughout the world. And he sees ways in which he can help advance technology and change people's lives. He looks around him and sees possibilities. And as his mother found out all those years ago, he is thinking, always thinking.

THE U.S. GOVERNMENT V. MICROSOFT

AS FOUNDER AND CHAIRMAN of the world's most successful computer company, Bill Gates has grown used to criticism. His vision of a computer in every home has partly come true. But along with this vision has come criticism of the man behind the technology. He is seen by some as a power-hungry businessperson who is trying to capture the entire computer market for his company. Fear of the new technology, which few people really understood, and disapproval of some of his business practices has led many people to become suspicious of Microsoft's founder. More than any other person, Bill Gates has become the face of the new computer industry—for better and for worse. Eventually, the federal government joined the chorus of vocal critics, investigating Gates's business methods.

What Is a Monopoly?

Some of the criticism aimed at Gates was the result of the quick success of Microsoft. This is similar to the reactions to other great American tycoons. In the nineteenth century, newspapers published cartoon drawings of fat industrialists walking over the landscape and towering over ordinary people. Men like Andrew Carnegie, the steel magnate, were ridiculed for their acquisition of money and power. Their wealth and influence frightened and awed people, sometimes because they abused their position. Most of all, these men of industry were criticized for crushing those who stood in their way and for using their money and influence to stop other companies from competing with them. A law, called the Sherman Anti-Trust Act, was passed to ensure fair competition in the United States

When one company controls an entire industry,

it is said to have a *monopoly*. When one company establishes a monopoly, no one else can compete, and the people who buy whatever the company makes are at the mercy of that one company. In other words, a monopoly allows a company to charge whatever price it wants. For example, if one company owned all the dairy farms in the United States, it could charge whatever price it wished for milk. Everyone who went to the supermarket for a gallon of milk would have to buy the one kind of milk for sale at whatever price the monopoly decided to charge. They would have no choice.

To protect that lucrative position, companies who enjoy monopolies use heavy-handed tactics. For example, if an independent dairy farmer decided to sell the milk from his own cows to the stores, the giant milk monopoly could threaten to pull its own products from the store. ("If you buy his milk you can no longer sell my milk," the monopoly might say to the grocer, "and you will lose business.") Or, the giant milk monopoly could try to buy the independent dairy farmer's business for much less than it is worth. Even so, the farmer might even make money selling his small farm to the monopoly, but the monopoly would once again have complete control of the milk market.

The federal government decided that this kind of business practice was unfair and un-American. The government said that competition is at the heart of the U.S. economy. People should have a fair chance to start new businesses that would be able to compete with the giant companies. This competition also gives the consumer a choice. To prevent companies from establishing monopolies, the government passed antitrust laws, which allow the government to break monopolies and punish, usually through fines, the companies that create a monopoly.

Is Microsoft a Monopoly?

In the United States, business competition must be fair. A company that unfairly limits competition, whether it means to or not, can be punished for violating the antitrust laws.

Bill Gates had always dreamed of owning the most successful computer company in the world. From the early days of building computers in the garage, Microsoft grew into one of the world's richest companies. In addition, Microsoft became the center of a new economy based on computer technology.

Gates testifying before a congressional committee in 1998. He has had to answer many questions about Microsoft and its practices.

The U.S. economy was undergoing a rapid change and the demand for the new technology skyrocketed. Bill Gates had worked on this dream for his entire career, and it was paying off beyond anyone's expectations. Along the way, however, Gates attracted the attention of the Justice Department. Its lawyers were responsible for making sure that companies did not establish monopolies.

Because Microsoft products became so popular, they were the standard operating programs for most computers. Consumers loved the Windows design—the little boxes that open up on the computer screen. This was good news for Bill Gates, but bad news for his competition. Competitors began to complain of the hostile business practices of Microsoft. Some companies complained that they could not break into the market because Microsoft was keeping them out unfairly.

A couple of key points were brought out in these complaints. First, small companies often claimed that Microsoft bought up their products to keep them out of the stores. The second complaint was that Microsoft had unfairly cornered the market for web browsers. The World Wide Web had become popular in an astonishingly short period of time.

The number of websites went from just a few in the early 1990s to hundreds of thousands by the year 2000. The Internet became so popular that companies in a wide range of businesses started to sell their goods on-line, or electronically.

U.S. companies jumped into the Internet explosion with astonishing speed. Even industries that usually act slowly and with great caution, such as banking, entered the new electronic marketplace. It is now possible to have an on-line bank account and pay bills without having to buy stamps or walk to the mailbox.

The gateway to the electronic marketplace is the Internet browser, which gives the computer user access to various websites. To capitalize on this new market, Microsoft included its own web browser with its Windows operating system. With this marketing strategy, Microsoft got the lion's share of the browser market, and soon other companies were crying foul. They also claimed that Microsoft was forcing computer manufacturers to keep competing browsers from being installed.

Lawyers from the Justice Department and attorneys for individual states sued Microsoft for violating the antitrust laws. The legal case will have profound effects on Microsoft and perhaps on the future of America's leading industry.

Gates defended Microsoft's strategy. He argued that his company had created the Internet revolution that was beneficial for the U.S. economy and which has led to soaring stock prices for computer-related companies. To punish Microsoft, Gates argued, would be like punishing an inventor for his own invention. Others say that no one person or company is responsible for the Internet revolution and that Gates is arrogant and his practices are unlawful.

The Court Ruling

On April 3, 2000, a federal judge announced the conclusions of the U.S. case against Microsoft. Judge Thomas Penfield Jackson said that Microsoft had violated U.S. antitrust laws and unfairly squashed competition. He ruled that Microsoft's Windows operating system was designed to exclude other products and that by tying the web browser to the Windows applications, Microsoft had created a monopoly. According to the *New York Times*, the judge ruled that Microsoft made "a deliberate and purposeful choice to quell incipient competition,"

Gates addressing reporters after the April 2000 ruling against Microsoft

and that marketing of its Web browser represented "part of a larger campaign to quash innovation." So the ascendancy of Microsoft and its hold on the U.S. market for personal computers was found to be unfair by the federal government. The federal judge went so far as to accuse Microsoft of doing "violence to the competitive process," surely a damning accusation in a country whose economy is based on competition.

The day after the court ruling, Bill Gates was walking slowly through the corridors of Congress in a somber blue suit. He talked with lawmakers and went to the White House, where he chatted with President Clinton in his usual soft-spoken manner. As he spoke, he helped outline the future of personal computing. His infectious optimism was unchecked by the recent ruling and his audience listened attentively. They were aware that this man knew much more about the future of the computer industry than they did. Gates was visiting Washington at the invitation of President Clinton. He was summoned to speak at the White House conference on the new economy. And everyone there knew that Bill Gates was as responsible as any other person for creating that new economy.

Gates and Microsoft appealed the April ruling, but on June 7, 2000, they got very bad news. A U.S. district court judge ruled that Microsoft was to be broken up. Under the order, the company would become two separate companies that actually would

With President Clinton (right) at a White House conference. Gates and Microsoft continue to have great impact on the world economy.

compete against one another. One company would handle all Windows products and operating systems. The other would concentrate on computer programs and Internet businesses. Also, Microsoft would have to accept a long list of operating restrictions. The court would monitor the company's business behavior for a number of years.

Gates called the judge's ruling "an unwarranted and unjustified intrusion into the software marketplace, a marketplace that has been an engine of economic growth for America."

On June 13, Microsoft filed an appeal to this ruling. Steve Ballmer explained, "Microsoft is looking forward to the next phase of this case, and we are optimistic that the appellate courts will reverse the recent ruling. Obviously, we will comply with any final order in this case, but we believe this judgment is both wrong and unfair. We believe the appellate courts will recognize that Microsoft's product innovation is the heart and soul of competition in the high-tech industry."

In response to this appeal, the government announced that it wished to take the issue directly to the Supreme Court. But it remained unclear what direction the case will take next.

A Vision of the Future

Gates has said that he will continue to fight for Microsoft. He has also tried to appear unworried about the future. In April 2000, he launched an advertising campaign on television, in which he trumpeted the benefits of computers for business and individuals. In the ads, Gates sounds optimistic. "The best is yet to come," he promises. He has always been a dreamer, with his mind scurrying off in all sorts of interesting directions. The question now for Bill Gates and for Microsoft is what to do next.

Gates's Vision

Society today is heavily reliant on computers, but Gates envisions a future in which even more of our daily lives will be affected by computer technology. Take the book for example. "Reading on paper is so much a part of our lives that it is hard to imagine anything could ever replace inky marks on shredded trees," Gates wrote in an article in the weekly magazine *The Economist*. But he argues that printing on paper was the only option in the past.

Today, he says, other alternatives exist. The e-book, for example, is a hand-held computer that contains the entire text of a book and can be read directly from the computer's monitor. (Perhaps you are reading this on an e-book!) Gates sees great potential for electronic books and argues that they could even make people's lives better. "It is hard to imagine today," he wrote, "but one of the greatest contributions of e-books may eventually be in improving literacy and education in less-developed countries." In the future, he argues, e-books will be much cheaper than printing on paper. "It will be possible to set up 'virtual' public libraries which will have access to the same content as the Library of Congress," he wrote, referring to the largest library in the United States.

The potential of e-books is just one example of Gates's vision for the role of computers. He sees himself as something of a pioneer, forging ahead into the unknown. Bill Gates has always liked stories of great inventors, of American pioneers who changed the country through their curiosity and hard work.

Two inventors he particularly admires are the Wright brothers. Wilbur and Orville Wright owned a bicycle shop, but dreamed of inventing a new means of transportation. They fiddled with the parts from

Gates with third-grade schoolchildren in East Palo Alto, California

their bicycle workshop and drew plans for a flying machine. In 1903, the Wright brothers successfully launched the first machine-powered airplane, and forever changed the world. Reflecting on the Wright brothers, Gates noted: "The twentieth century has been the American Century in large part because of great inventors such as the Wright brothers." Gates, too, has earned his place among great American inventors, and his inventions have changed the way we live.

TIMELINE

1955	William H. Gates III born on October 28 in Seattle, Washington
1971	Begins a company called Traf-O-Data with friend Paul Allen
1972	Spends the summer in Washington, D.C., working as a congressional page
1973	Graduates from Lakeside; begins freshman year at Harvard University
1975	Writes first software program; forms Microsoft in Albuquerque with partner Paul Allen
1977	Leaves Harvard
1979	Microsoft moves to Bellevue, Washington
1980	The SoftCard introduced; Microsoft forms partnership with IBM
1981	MS-DOS released

1983	Paul Allen resigns from Microsoft; Windows announced; Word announced for MS-DOS
1986	Microsoft moves to Redmond, Washington; Microsoft goes public
1987	Becomes the United States' youngest billionaire
1988	Windows 2.0 released
1990	Windows 3.0 released
1992	Receives the National Medal of Technology for Technological Achievement
1993	Microsoft Encarta introduced; Mouse 2.0 software introduced
1994	Marries Melinda French
1995	Windows 95 introduced; publishes *The Road Ahead*
1996	Daughter Jennifer Katherine born
1997	Announces a collaboration with Apple
1998	Windows 98 introduced
1999	Publishes *Business @ the Speed of Thought*; son, Rory John, born
2000	Steps down as CEO of Microsoft to concentrate on software development

HOW TO BECOME A COMPUTER PROGRAMMER

The Job

Computer programmers work in the field of electronic data processing. They write instructions that tell computers what to do in a computer language, or code, that the computer understands. Systems programmers specialize in maintaining the general instructions that control an entire computer system. Maintenance tasks include giving computers instructions on how to allocate time to various jobs they receive from computer terminals and making sure that these assignments are performed properly. There are approximately 648,000 computer programmers employed in the United States.

Broadly speaking, there are two types of computer programmers: systems programmers and applications programmers. Systems programmers maintain the instructions, called programs or software, that control the entire computer system, including both the central processing unit and the equipment with which it communicates, such as terminals, printers, and disk drives. Applications programmers write the software to handle specific jobs and may specialize as engineering and scientific programmers or as business programmers. Some of the latter specialists may be designated chief business programmers, who supervise the work of other business programmers.

Programmers are often given program specifications, prepared by systems analysts, which list in detail the steps the computer must follow in order to complete a given task. Programmers then code these instructions in a computer language the computer understands. In smaller companies, analysis and programming may be handled by the same person, called a programmer-analyst.

Before actually writing the computer program, a programmer must analyze the work request, understand the current problem and desired resolution, decide on an approach to the problem, and plan what the machine will have to do to produce the required results. Programmers prepare a flowchart to show the steps in sequence that the machine must make. They must pay attention to minute detail and instruct the machine in each step of the process.

These instructions are then coded in one of several programming languages, such as BASIC, COBOL, FORTRAN, PASCAL, RPG, CSP, or C++. When the program is completed, the programmer tests its working practicality by running it on simulated data. If the machine responds according to expectations, actual data will be fed into it and the program will be activated. If the computer does not respond as anticipated, the program will have to be debugged—that is, examined for errors that must be eliminated. Finally, the programmer prepares an instruction sheet for the computer operator who will run the program.

The programmer's job concerns both an overall picture of the problem at hand and the minute detail of potential solutions. Programmers work from two points of view: from that of the people who need certain results and from that of technological problem solving. The work is divided equally between meeting the needs of other people and comprehending the capabilities of the machines.

Electronic data systems involve more than just one machine. Depending upon the kind of system being used, the operation may require other machines such as printers or other peripherals. Introducing a new piece of equipment to an existing system often requires programmers to rewrite many programs.

Process control programmers develop programs for systems that control automatic operations for commercial and industrial enterprises, such as steelmaking, sanitation plants, combustion systems, computerized production testing, or automatic truck loading. Numerical control tool programmers program the tape that controls the machining of automatic machine tools.

Requirements

High School In high school, you should take any computer programming or computer science courses available. You should also concentrate on math, science, and schematic drawing courses, since these subjects directly prepare students for careers in computer programming.

Postsecondary Most employers prefer their programmers to be college graduates. In the past, as the field was first taking shape, employers were known to hire people with some formal education and little or no experience but determination and aptitude to learn quickly. As the market becomes saturated with individuals wishing to break into this field, however, a college degree is becoming increasingly important.

Many personnel officers administer aptitude tests to determine potential for programming work. Some employers send new employees to computer schools or in-house training sessions before they are considered qualified to assume programming responsibilities. Training periods may last as long as a few weeks, months, or even a year.

Many junior and community colleges also offer two-year associate's degree programs in data processing, computer programming, and other computer-related technologies.

Most four-year colleges and universities have computer science departments with a variety of computer-related majors, any of which could prepare a student for a career in programming. Employers who require a college degree often do not express a preference as to major field of study, although mathematics or computer science is highly favored. Other acceptable majors may be business administration, accounting, engineering, or physics. Entrance requirements for jobs with the government are much the same as those in private industry.

Licensing and Certification   Students who choose to obtain a two-year degree might consider becoming certified by the Institute for Certification of Computing Professionals. (See "To Learn More about Computer Programmers" for contact information.) Although it is not required, certification may boost an individual's attractiveness to employers during the job search.

Other Requirements Personal qualifications such as a high degree of reasoning ability, patience, and persistence, as well as aptitude for mathematics, are important for computer programmers. Some employers whose work is highly technical require that programmers be qualified in the area in which the firm or agency operates. Engineering firms, for example, prefer young people with an engineering background and are willing to train them in some programming techniques. For other firms, such as banks, consumer-level knowledge of the services that they offer may be sufficient background for incoming programmers.

Exploring

If you are interested in becoming a computer programmer, you might visit a large bank or insurance company in the community and seek an appointment to talk with one of the programmers on the staff. You may be able to visit the data processing center and see the machines in operation. You might also talk with a sales representative from one of the large manufacturers of data processing equipment and request whatever brochures or pamphlets the company publishes.

It is a good idea to start early and get some hands-on experience operating and programming a computer. A trip to the local library or bookstore is likely to turn up countless books on programming; this is one field where the resources to teach yourself are highly accessible and available for all levels of competency. Joining a computer club and reading professional magazines are other ways to become more familiar with this career field. In addition, you should start exploring the Internet, itself a great source of information about computer-related careers.

High school and college students who can operate a computer may be able to obtain part-time jobs in business computer centers or in some larger companies. Any computer experience will be helpful for future computer training.

Employers

Computer programmers work for manufacturing companies, data processing service firms, hardware and software companies, banks, insurance companies, credit companies, publishing houses, government agencies, and colleges and universities throughout the country. Many programmers are employed by businesses as consultants on a temporary or contractual basis.

Starting Out

You can look for an entry-level programming position in the same way as most other jobs; there is no special or standard point of entry into the field. Individuals with the necessary qualifications should apply directly to companies, agencies, or industries that have announced job openings through a school placement office, an employment agency, or the classified ads.

Students in two- or four-year degree programs should work closely with their schools' placement offices, since major local employers often list job openings exclusively with such offices.

If the market for programmers is particularly tight, you may want to obtain an entry-level job with a large corporation or computer software firm, even if the job does not include programming. As jobs in the programming department open up, current employees in other departments are often the first to know, and are favored over nonemployees during the interviewing process. Getting a foot in the door in this way has proven to be successful for many programmers.

Advancement

Programmers are ranked—according to education, experience, and level of responsibility—as junior or senior programmers. After programmers have attained the highest available programming position, they can choose to make one of several career moves in order to be promoted still higher.

Some programmers are more interested in the analysis aspect of computing than the actual charting and coding of programming. They often acquire additional training and experience in order to prepare themselves for promotion to positions as systems programmers or systems analysts. These individuals have the added responsibility of working with upper management to define equipment and cost guidelines for a specific project. They perform only broad programming tasks, leaving most of the detail work to programmers.

Other programmers become more interested in administration and management and may wish to become heads of programming departments. They tend to be more people-oriented and enjoy leading others to excellence. As the level of management responsibilities increases, the amount of technical work performed decreases, so management positions are not for everyone.

Still other programmers may branch out into different technical areas, such as total computer operations, hardware design, and software or network engineering. With experience, they may be placed in charge of the data systems center. They may also decide to go to work for a consulting company, work that generally pays extremely well.

Earnings

According to the National Association of Colleges and Employers, the average 1999 starting salary for college graduates employed in the private sector was about $40,800. The U.S. Department of Labor reports that median annual earnings for computer programmers were $47,550 in 1998. The lowest 10 percent of programmers earned $27,760, while the highest 10 percent earned more than $88,730 annually. Programmers in the West and the Northeast are generally paid more than those in the South and Midwest. This is because most big computer companies are located in northern California's Silicon Valley or in the state of Washington, where Microsoft, a major employer of programmers, has its headquarters. Also, some industries, like public utilities and data processing service firms, tend to pay their programmers higher wages than do other types of employers, such as banks and schools.

Work Environment

Most programmers work in pleasant office conditions, since computers require an air-conditioned, dust-free environment. Programmers perform most of their duties in one primary location but may be asked to travel to other computing sites on occasion.

The average programmer works between 35 and 40 hours weekly. In some job situations, the programmer may have to work nights or weekends on short notice. This might happen when a program is going through its trial runs, for example, or when there are many demands for additional services.

Outlook

Employment opportunities for computer programmers should increase faster than the average through 2008, according to the U.S. Department of Labor. Employment growth will be strong because businesses, scientific organizations, government agencies, and schools continue to look for new applications for computers and to make improvements in software already in use. Also, there is a need to develop complex operating programs that can use higher-level computer languages and can network with other computer equipment and systems.

Job applicants with the best chances of employment will be college graduates with a knowledge of several programming languages, especially newer ones used for computer networking and database management. In addition, the best applicants will have some training or experience in an applied field such as accounting, science, engineering, or management. Competition for jobs will be heavier among graduates of two-year data processing programs and among people with equivalent experience or with less training. Since this field is constantly changing, programmers should stay abreast of the latest technology to remain competitive.

TO LEARN MORE ABOUT COMPUTER PROGRAMMERS

Books

Gascoigne, Marc. *You Can Surf the Net: Your Guide to the World of the Internet*. New York: Puffin, 1996.

Lampton, Christopher. *Home Page: An Introduction to Web Page Design*. Danbury, Conn.: Franklin Watts, 1997.

Lund, Bill. *Getting Ready for a Career in Computers*. Mankato, Minn.: Capstone Press, 1998.

Pedersen, Ted. *Make Your Own Web Page!: A Guide for Kids*. New York: Price Stern Sloan, 1998.

Perry, Robert. *Personal Computer Communications*. Danbury, Conn.: Franklin Watts, 2000.

Reeves, Diane Lindsey. *Career Ideas for Kids Who Like Computers*. New York: Facts On File, 1998.

Websites

The Computer Museum History Center
http://www.computerhistory.org/
Online archives and exhibits about the history of computers

PC World Online
http://www.pcworld.com
An online magazine that provides news about the computer industry as well as reviews of software and other products

Programmers Heaven
http://www.programmersheaven.com
An online source for computer programmers with all levels of experience

Where to Write

Association for Computing Machinery
One Astor Plaza
1515 Broadway
New York, NY 10036
ACMHELP@acm.org
For more information about careers in computer programming

Institute for Certification of Computing Professionals
2200 East Devon Avenue, Suite 247
Des Plaines, IL 60018
For information on certification programs

HOW TO BECOME AN ENTREPRENEUR

The Job

Have you ever baby-sat neighborhood kids? Mowed a lawn or two in the summer? Then you already know something about being an entrepreneur. You've set your own hours, named your prices, and raked in the dough. Or something like that. The entrepreneurial spirit has long been strong in kids and teens; this is evident in the number of junior achievement organizations, such as Future Business Leaders of America (FBLA), devoted to the interests of young entrepreneurs. A Gallup poll found that 70 percent of high school seniors want to own their own businesses someday.

Though entrepreneurial enterprises have long been popular with teenagers, people often outgrow the ambition to embark on their own businesses. If you start a small business while still living at home you have a bit less to lose—you don't have a family to support, a life-long savings to wipe out, or rent due. But many adults ignore the risks of entrepreneurship. Some of the biggest corporations of today started out as small businesses: Coca-Cola was a concoction by a Georgian pharmacist who jugged his mixture in his backyard, then carried it to Jacob's Pharmacy to sell for a nickel a glass. And it seems there are even more entrepreneurial success stories today. Dineh Mohager invented Hard Candy cosmetics by mixing nail polishes together, gave the colors mock-exploitative names like Scam and Skitzo, and made gross sales of more than $10 million her first year of business. Dave Kapell invented Magnetic Poetry and now pulls in $6 million a year in sales.

But you don't have to invent a new fashion trend or popular novelty to strike out on your own. Though the numbers vary from study to study, the American Association of Home-Based Businesses (AAHBB) reports that there are more than 24 million home-based businesses in the United States. Some of these businesses may be making big money, but most are simply making their founders comfortable. In addition to providing services and making good living wages, many small business owners are fulfilling their dreams. For example, a personal chef may find the slower pace of creating individualized menus much more satisfying than the odd hours and frantic demands of a restaurant kitchen. A husband and wife may gladly quit their full-time jobs to open up their home as a bed and breakfast.

Owning a small business has been part of the American dream since the earliest days of the country, and the late twentieth century saw a great increase in entrepreneurial ambition. This may be in part because of the downsizing trends of American companies. Whereas earlier in the twentieth century, a person could work for one company until retirement, such job security has become more rare. It's increasingly common for men and women in their fifties to lose their jobs, and find themselves with few job prospects. With severance pay in hand, these people often invest in the businesses they've been longing for, recognizing these ventures as no more risky than any other career pursuit. Once upon a time, a person chose a job path and stuck with it; these days, people experiment with a variety of careers throughout their lives.

There are more than 400 colleges and universities that offer entrepreneurship courses—200 more than there were in 1984. There are also more organizations, periodicals, and Web pages advising people on how to start their own businesses and keep them running. *Entrepreneur* and *Success* magazines publish special issues devoted to small business and maintain Websites. The Edward Lowe Foundation gives small business owners access to extensive databases, research, and conferences and publishes *Entrepreneurial Edge* magazine. The Small Business Administration (SBA) guarantees more than $10 billion in loans every year; 24 percent of the loans from the SBA's largest program go to minority-owned businesses. The SBA also provides business start-up kits, workshops, and research assistance.

This wealth of information, along with the ease of accessing it via the Internet, has undoubtedly played a part in the boom in small business. Technology in general has made it easier to run your own business from home. Computer software, specially designed for your profession, takes much of the time and effort away from administrative details. E-mail and fax allows you better communication, and the Internet puts you in touch with market research, industry support, and ways to better promote your business.

Structure

While there are a lot of resources to help you get your business started, there are also a lot of things you have to figure out about yourself first. Do you have the personal characteristics necessary for running a successful business? You'll need self-motivation for making contacts, pursuing clients and projects, and getting the work done—you won't have a supervisor giving you deadlines and checking your work. You'll also need dedication; it may be easy in the early days of the business to give up when the going gets rough, but you have to keep in mind that a new business can take a few years to get off the ground. Self-confidence is also important, because you'll be marketing yourself and your talents. And because the work may not be steady, you must be good at budgeting money for the lean months.

Once you've decided that you're up to the task of small business ownership, you'll need to consider the pros and cons of entrepreneurship. Depending on the nature of your business, you'll have the freedom to set your own hours, keep your own schedule, and possibly work at home. But you'll only get paid when you're actually doing work—you won't get vacation pay or sick leave. You also won't get company health benefits or a retirement plan. The success of your business will be based mostly on your own efforts—this can be both a plus and a minus. While you can take full credit for your success, you also must do all the work yourself. If you are working for a company, there are receptionists to answer the phones, accountants to handle the finances, and advertising departments to promote the company, while you can focus on your own assignments. But with your own business, you may have to take responsibility for every aspect of its operation, from finding clients to billing them. You also need to keep in mind that about one-half of all small businesses fail. You may want to explore a college entrepreneurship program. Many business schools are offering courses in entrepreneurship; these courses, and whole entrepreneurship programs, have gained a great deal of popularity in the last 10 years. Often these courses are led by people who have started their own successful businesses.

Still ready for self-employment? First, you'll need to choose what your business will be. You may want to work in a field already familiar to you, a business in which you'll be able to use your talents and professional contacts. You'll definitely want to choose something you're interested in. But some people embark on businesses they know little about—those who have the money to invest in successful franchises like McDonald's or Dairy Queen may only be interested in the big profits promised by the franchisers. But, if you're like most people, you'll be starting your business on a shoestring and expanding later.

After you've decided on your business, you'll begin to do research. You'll contact professional organizations, chambers of commerce, the SBA, and other organizations to learn about the industry and marketplace. You'll read industry reports and magazine articles, visit Websites, maybe even attend trade shows and conferences. You'll interview other entrepreneurs. You'll also find out what licenses and certification you'll need to obtain. In the research stage, you may learn that there's not enough money to be made, or that there are too many similar businesses in your area, or that there's not much of a future in the field. Or you may find out that there's great demand for such a business and that there's a lot of small business support within the industry. If your research is encouraging, you'll start to develop your new business. This may be as simple as investing in some software and making some calls. But, in most cases, it will be much more intensive. Experts recommend a business plan, which involves defining your business, setting goals, and predicting income. Not only will the business plan be needed in getting loans, but it will help you keep your plans in focus. It will also help you determine what equipment and staffing you'll need. The American Home Business Association (AHBA) and the SBA are a few of the organizations that can help you develop a business plan.

"Niche" marketing is an important aspect of any business's success. What will set your business apart from others? How will you attract customers to the unique qualities of your product or service? This is where your originality and imagination come in. Figuring out what makes your business special, determining its niche, will help you promote your business and secure loans and other financial backing.

Now we're at the tricky part—where's your initial investment money going to come from? Even if you don't need much equipment and promotion to get started, you'll need money in the bank for operating expenses, including your own salary. Before starting your business, make sure you have enough money to get by for at least the first year. Some people get started with their own savings or with severance pay from former employers. A few others have spouses who work full-time and can provide additional security. Many develop their own businesses part-time, while still employed. Some get loans from a bank, the SBA, or a commercial finance company. But others simply leap in, without money or plans, hoping to solicit enough business to pay the bills for a while.

Despite all the careful planning and research advised by business experts, there are many people who stumble onto their own entrepreneurial success. Dineh Mohager, the founder of Hard Candy, was a medical student when she sold her first bottle of nail polish to a local department store. Dave Kapell was a musician and songwriter when he invented Magnetic Poetry. No matter whether you just jump into the world of self-employment or you map out a detailed business plan, some very important elements for every small business owner are good luck and great timing, factors difficult to depend upon.

Outlook

Despite some discouraging statistics that put small business failure at 50 percent, the number of entrepreneurial ventures will only increase. The majority of business school graduates will make their careers with entrepreneurships, either by starting their own businesses or by hiring on with small business owners. With a number of professional organizations and the SBA devoted to small business, the new entrepreneur can find a great deal of support—technical, financial, and emotional.

TO LEARN MORE ABOUT ENTREPRENEURS

Books

Bernstein, Daryl. *Better Than a Lemonade Stand: Small Business Ideas for Kids*. Hillsborough, Ore.: Beyond Words, 1992.

Erlbach, Arlene. *The Kids' Business Book*. Minneapolis: Lerner, 1998.

Greenberg, Keith Elliot. *Bowerman and Knight: Building the Nike Empire*. Woodbridge, Conn.: Blackbirch Press, 1997.

Haskins, Jim. *African American Entrepreneurs*. Black Star Series. New York: Wiley, 1998.

Merrill, Jean. *The Toothpaste Millionaire*. New York: Houghton Miffin, 1999.

Nelson, Sharlene. *William Boeing: Builder of Planes*. Danbury, Conn.: Children's Press, 1999.

Older, Jules. *Anita!: The Woman behind the Body Shop*. Watertown, Mass.: Charlesbridge, 1998.

Websites
EntrepreneurMag.com
http://www.entrepreneurmag.com
Articles and tools for the entrepreneur

Forum for Women Entrepreneurs
http://www.fwe.org
A group that supports and promotes entrepreneurship for women in technology and health care businesses

Where to Write
American Association of Home-Based Businesses
P.O. Box 10023
Rockville, MD 20849
To learn about membership support and other benefits
Edward Lowe Foundation
58220 Decatur Road, P.O. Box 8
Cassopolis, MI 49031-0008
For information about *Entrepreneurial Edge* magazine and many other small business resources

National Association of Women Business Owners
1411 K Street
Washington, DC 20005
national@nawbo.org
To learn about membership for women entrepreneurs

U.S. Small Business Administration
409 3rd Street, S.W.
Washington DC 20416
For small business statistics and other relevant information

TO LEARN MORE ABOUT BILL GATES

Books

Connolly, Sean. *Bill Gates: An Unauthorized Biography.* Portsmouth, N.H.: Heinemann, 1998.

Dickinson, Joan D. *Bill Gates: Billionaire Computer Genius.* Springfield, N.J.: Enslow Publishers, 1997.

Forman, Michael. *Bill Gates: Software Billionaire.* New York: Crestwood House, 1998.

Simon, Charnan. *Bill Gates: Helping People Use Computers.* Community Builders. Danbury, Conn.: Children's Press, 1997.

Woog, Adam. *Bill Gates.* San Diego: Lucent Books, 1998.

Websites

Bill and Melinda Gates Foundation

http://www.gatesfoundations.org/

Provides details about their charitable giving and world-wide programs.

Microsoft

http://www.microsoft.com/

For the latest in Microsoft products and activities. Internet site offers a biography of Gates and a corporate timeline.

Interesting Places to Visit

Ben and Jerry's Ice Cream Factory

30 Community Drive
South Burlington, VT 05403-6828
802/882-1240

The Computer Museum of America

Coleman College
7380 Parkway Drive
La Mesa, CA 91942
619/465-8226

The NYSE Interactive Education Center

New York Stock Exchange
20 Broad Street, 3rd Floor
New York, NY 10005
212/656-5165

INDEX

Page numbers in *italics* indicate illustrations.

Allen, Paul, *17*, 19, 28,
  30–32, 34–35, 48–49, 64
Altair 8800 computer, 28–29,
  29, 31–32
Apple Computer, 38, 47, 58,
  60, 76

Ballmer, Steve, 27, 40–41,
  64, 80, 82, *89*, 96
BallPoint Mouse, 61
BASIC programming language,
  18, 30, 32, 38, 103
Bill and Melinda Gates Foun-
  dation, 77, 79
*Business @ the Speed of
  Thought* (book), 80, *81*, 82

computer programmers
  aptitude testing, 106
  average salaries for, 110
  career advancement,
    109–110
  career exploration, 107–108
  certification, 106
  educational requirements,
    105–106
  employers of, 108
  employment outlook for, 111
  work environment, 110–111
computers, *8*, 9–10, *10*, *11*,
  13, 41, *46*
Corporate Campus, 49, *50*, 51

disk operating systems (DOS),
  45

Encarta multimedia software,
  61

entrepreneurs
    business selection, 118
    employment outlook for, 120
    investment money, 119
    "niche" marketing, 119
    structure of, 116

FORTRAN programming
    language, 34, 103
French, Melinda. *See* Gates,
    Melinda.

Gates, Jennifer Katherine
    (daughter), 75
Gates, Kristi (sister), 15
Gates, Libby (sister), 15, *15*
Gates, Mary (mother), 15
Gates, Melinda (wife), 64, *65*,
    75, *78*
Gates, Rory John (son), 75
Gates, William H. III, *17*, *51*,
    58, *71*, *78*, *89*, *93*
    birth of, 13
    as business leader, 52–54
    *Business @ the Speed of
        Thought* (book), 80, *81*, 82
    charitable works of, 77, 79,
        82
    childhood of, 15–16, 20, 54
    education of, 16, 23, 25, 27
    government investigation
        of, 86, *93*
    graduation from Lakeside,
        23, *23*
    at Harvard University, 23,
        25, *26*

Lakeside Programmers
    Group, 18
marriage to Melinda French,
    64
media coverage of, *55*, 66
in Microsoft advertising
    campaign, 97
National Medal of Technol-
    ogy award, 62, *63*, 64
President's Medal Leader-
    ship Award, 80
Road Ahead, The (book),
    72
at White House economic
    conference, 94
Gates, William, Jr. (father), 13,
    14
Graham, Katherine, 66

hacking, 19
Harvard University, 23

International Business
    Machines (IBM), 41, *42*,
    43, 57
Internet, 9, 72, 79, 121. *See
    also* World Wide Web.
Internet Explorer, 72

Jackson, Thomas Penfield, 92,
    94
Jobs, Steve, *39*, 40, 47, *47*, 77

Kapell, Dave, 115, 119

Lakeside School, 16, *17*, 23

Macintosh computers, 58
Microsoft Corporation, 31–32,
  34–35, 37–38
  advertising campaign for, 97
  antitrust law violations, 88,
    91–92, 94
  Apple Computer lawsuit
    against, 60
  BallPoint Mouse, 61
  at Corporate Campus, 49,
    50, 51
  DreamWorks SKG and, 70
  employees, 51–52, *51*, *52*,
    53
  Federal Trade Commission
    investigation of, 60
  IBM and, 41, 43, 57
  international sales expan-
    sion, 38
  Internet Explorer, 72
  media coverage of, 61, 92
  Microsoft Network, 72
  as a monopoly, 87–88, 92
  Money, *62*
  Mouse 2.0, 61
  operating restrictions, 96
  OS/2 operating system, 57
  partnership with Apple
    Computer, 76–77
  split of, 95–96
  Windows operating sys-
    tems, 57–58, 70, 72, *73*,
    76, 90–92
  Word, 48
Microsoft Money, *62*

Microsoft Network, 72
Microsoft Word, 48
MITS (Micro-Instrumentation
  and Telemetry Systems),
  28–29, 31
Mouse 2.0, 61
MS-DOS operating system,
  45

OS/2 operating system, 57–58

programming languages
  BASIC, 18, 30, 38, 104
  debugging, 104
  FORTRAN, 34, 104
  hacking, 19

Scully, John, *47*
Seattle Computer Products,
  44–45
Sherman Anti-Trust Act, 86
Spielberg, Steven, *71*

Winblad, Ann, 68, *69*
Windows operating systems,
  48, *59*, 90–92
  Windows 2.0, 57–58
  Windows 3.0, 58
  Windows 95, 70, 72, *73*
  Windows 98, 76
  Windows 2000, 76
World Wide Web, 90–91. *See
  also* Internet.
Wozniak, Steve, 40, *47*

ABOUT THE AUTHOR

Lucia Raatma received her bachelor's degree in English literature from the University of South Carolina and her master's degree in cinema studies from New York University. Both degrees taught her the power of stories, and very often she feels that the best stories are true ones. She found Bill Gates' life to be an amazing example of determination and confidence.

Lucia Raatma has written a wide range of books for young people. They include *Libraries* and *How Books Are Made* (Children's Press); an eight-book general safety series and a four-book fire safety series (Bridgestone Books); fourteen titles in a character education series (Bridgestone Books); and a forthcoming biography of Margaret Mead (Franklin Watts). She has also written career biographies of Charles Lindbergh and Maya Angelou for this series.

When she is not researching or writing, she enjoys going to movies, playing tennis, and spending time with her husband, daughter, and golden retriever.